JUV
808.1
M

14 Day

D1217328

Poet's Workshop

Read, Recite, and Write

NARRATIVE POEMS

Leodogra   ... King of Cameliard,
Had one fair dau ... er, and none other child;
And she was the fa ... est of all flesh on earth,
Guinevere, and in her his one delight.

JoAnn
Early
Macken

POET'S WORKSHOP

Author
JoAnn Early Macken

Publishing plan research and development
Reagan Miller

Project coordinator
Kelly Spence

Editor
Anastasia Suen

Proofreader and indexer
Wendy Scavuzzo

Design
Margaret Amy Salter

Photo research
Margaret Amy Salter

Prepress technician
Margaret Amy Salter

Print and production coordinator
Margaret Amy Salter

Photographs and illustrations
Wikimedia Commons: Zeichnugen von W.S. Gilbert: page
  4 (bottom), Jungpionier: page 4 (top); John Mueller: page
  10 (top); Aoara: page 10 (bottom); Palmer C. Hayden: page
  11; Dmitrismirnov: pages 22, 23
Other images by Shutterstock

JoAnn Early Macken is the author of *Write a Poem Step by Step*
(Earlybird Press), five picture books, and 125 nonfiction books for
young readers. Her poems appear in several children's magazines
and anthologies. JoAnn has taught writing at four Wisconsin
colleges. She speaks about poetry and writing to students,
teachers, and adult writers at schools, libraries, and conferences.
You can visit her website at www.joannmacken.com.

Library and Archives Canada Cataloguing in Publication

Macken, JoAnn Early, 1953-, author
       Read, recite, and write narrative poems / JoAnn Early
Macken.

(Poet's workshop)
Includes index.
Issued in print and electronic formats.
ISBN 978-0-7787-0410-2 (bound).--ISBN 978-0-7787-0414-0
(pbk.).--ISBN 978-1-4271-7522-9 (html).--ISBN 978-1-4271-7526-7
(pdf)

       1. Narrative poetry--Authorship--Juvenile literature.
I. Title.

PN6110.N17M35 2014   j808.1'3   C2014-900958-5
                                          C2014-900959-3

Library of Congress Cataloging-in-Publication Data

CIP available at Library of Congress

Crabtree Publishing Company

Printed in Canada/032014/BF20140212

www.crabtreebooks.com   1-800-387-7650

Published in Canada
Crabtree Publishing
616 Welland Ave.
St. Catharines, Ontario
L2M 5V6

Published in the United States
Crabtree Publishing
PMB 59051
350 Fifth Avenue, 59th Floor
New York, New York 10118

Published in the United Kingdom
Crabtree Publishing
Maritime House
Basin Road North, Hove
BN41 1WR

Published in Australia
Crabtree Publishing
3 Charles Street
Coburg North
VIC 3058

Contents

Chapter 1: What Is a Narrative Poem?

A **narrative** poem is a poem that tells a story. A story poem is two things at once. It is a story and it is a poem.

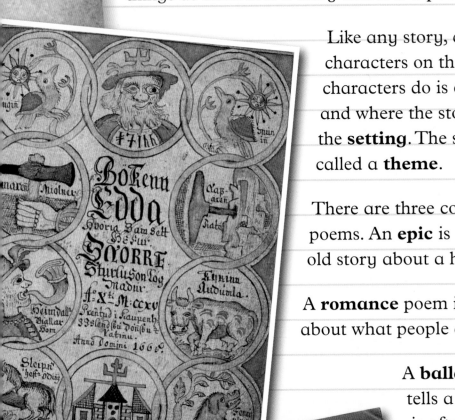

Like any story, a narrative poem has characters on the move. What those characters do is called the **plot**. When and where the story takes place is called the **setting**. The story also has a message, called a **theme**.

There are three common kinds of narrative poems. An **epic** is a long poem. It tells an old story about a hero.

A **romance** poem is also long. This poem is about what people do for love.

A **ballad** is a shorter poem that tells a story. This kind of poem is often told in a song. The examples you'll read in this book are ballads.

Prose vs. Drama vs. Poetry

In literature, we use different names to talk about the way words are used. The same story can be told in many different ways. You can see how in the examples below.

Prose

Once upon a time, there was a little boy. When he was a tiny baby, his father left. His father sailed far across the sea. The baby boy stayed home with his mother.

Drama

TIME: long ago
PLACE: a cottage in a town near the sea
[The SAILOR and his WIFE are standing at the door of the cottage.]
SAILOR: The sea is calling and I must go, dear wife.
WIFE: But your son was just born.
[Inside the cottage the BABY cries]
SAILOR: I have to provide for three now.
WIFE: We will wait for you, my love.

Poetry

Crowd about me, little children—
Come and cluster 'round my knee
While I tell a little story
That happened once with me.

My father he had gone away
A-sailing on the foam,
Leaving me - the merest infant -
And my mother dear at home. . . .
—James Whitcomb Riley

We use sentences to tell a story in **prose**. When a story is performed as a play, it is called a **drama**. Can you see the stage directions? They let the actors know when and where things happen.

The third example is a poem. A **poem** uses short **phrases**, or groups of words, to tell a story or share a feeling.

About This Book

In this book, you'll learn about one type of poem: the narrative poem.

Literature Links explore connections that all types of literature use.

Poetry Pointers explain the parts that are special to poetry.

Thinking Aloud sections include discussion questions, brainstorming tips, graphic organizers, and examples of students' writing.

Now It's Your Turn! gives you tips on how to write your very own narrative poems.

Five Steps to Writing

1. Pre-writing: Brainstorm new ideas. Write every one down, even if it seems as though it might not work.

2. Drafting: Your first copy can be sloppy. You can always fix it later.

3. Revising: Use input from other writers to make your poem better.

4. Editing: Check for spelling, grammar, and punctuation.

5. Publishing. Print and distribute your poem, give it as a gift, or publish it online.

The Song of Wandering Aengus

I went out to the hazel wood,
Because a fire was in my head,
And cut and peeled a hazel wand,
And hooked a berry to a thread;
And when white moths were on the wing,
And moth-like stars were flickering out,
I dropped the berry in a stream
And caught a little silver trout.

When I had laid it on the floor
I went to blow the fire a-flame,
But something rustled on the floor,
And someone called me by my name:
It had become a glimmering girl
With apple blossom in her hair
Who called me by my name and ran
And faded through the brightening air.

Though I am old with wandering
Through hollow lands and hilly lands,
I will find out where she has gone,
And kiss her lips and take her hands;
And walk among long dappled grass,
And pluck till time and times are done,
The silver apples of the moon,
The golden apples of the sun.

—William Butler Yeats

The Song of
Wandering Aengus

Stanza 1

Stanza 2

Stanza 3

Poetry Pointers: Stanzas

In prose, sentences are combined to form paragraphs. In a poem, lines are combined to form **stanzas**. "The Song of Wandering Aengus" is divided into three stanzas. That's three poetry paragraphs. In this poem, each stanza has eight lines.

Rhythm and Meter

Like the beat in music, the **rhythm** of a poem is a regular pattern of sound. A ballad can use any pattern of rhythm. "The Song of Wandering Aengus" has a regular rhythm that is easy to hear.

To **meter** means to measure. Poems with a regular rhythm are called metered or metric. To find the beat, or **stressed** syllables, tap or clap along as you read. You should feel the emphasis, or STRESS, on the syllables written in CAPITAL letters. This is what it looks like in the first four lines.

> i WENT out TO the HAzel WOOD,
> beCAUSE a FIRE was IN my HEAD,
> and CUT and PEELED a HAzel WAND,
> and HOOKED a BERry TO a THREAD....

Count the number of stresses in each line. You'll see that each line has four. Read the whole poem again and listen for its rhythm.

Notice the repeating two-syllable rhythm pattern in "i WENT out TO the HAzel WOOD." That da DUM da DUM pattern is common in narrative poems and speech.

Literature Link: Story Elements

Story elements include characters, setting, plot, and theme. Long narrative poems might describe these story elements in great detail. Shorter poems, as you will see in the examples, might barely touch on them.

Characters are the people, animals, or objects whose actions are described in a story. The **setting** includes both the place and the time that a story occurs. The plot includes the main events in a story. The theme is the main message of a story. It might be described in one word, such as "friendship" or "loyalty." To find the theme, read the poem carefully. Think about the meaning of the title, main events, and any patterns, symbols, or details.

Story Elements in "The Song of Wandering Aengus"

Character(s)	Unnamed first person narrator
Setting	Place Details: hazel wood, stream, floor (probably of the narrator's house), "hollow lands and hilly lands," "long dappled grass"
Time	Past **tense** verbs indicate the past; "I am old with wandering"
Plot	The narrator makes a fishing pole, goes fishing with a berry on a thread, and catches a fish. The fish turns into a girl who runs away. The narrator chases after her. What does he say he will do?
Theme	Some people believe the narrator is searching for his lost youth. What do you think?

Keep reading to find out how you can write your own narrative poem!

Chapter 2: Writing a Biographical Narrative Poem

There are many different types of stories. Some are make-believe and some are real. The story of someone's life is called a **biography**. That's what you will work on in this chapter. You will read, write, and recite poems that tell the story of someone's life.

Building the First Railroads

This story poem is about John Henry. He worked on the railroads when they were first being built. A mountain was a major barrier for the railroads. Workers had to blast through rock and soil with dynamite. To do that, first they had to make a hole for the dynamite.

Two men worked together as a team. They pounded steel chisels with a large hammer called a sledgehammer. The man who held the hammer was called the "hammer man." The man who held the chisel was called a "shaker." The shaker shook the chisel to make the hole wider. Then he placed the dynamite in the hole.

There are many stories about the African American hero John Henry. Most of them are about this contest. John Henry raced against a steam-powered drilling machine.

Statues and old photographs can provide you with good ideas for describing characters in your poem.

John Henry

When John Henry was a little tiny baby
Sitting on his mama's knee,
He picked up a hammer and a little piece of steel
Saying, "Hammer's going to be the death of me,
 Lord, Lord,
Hammer's going to be the death of me."

John Henry was a man just six feet high,
Nearly two feet and a half across his chest.
He'd hammer with a nine-pound hammer all day
And never get tired and want to rest, Lord, Lord,
And never get tired and want to rest.

John Henry went up on the mountain
And he looked one eye straight up its side.
The mountain was so tall and John Henry was so small,
He laid down his hammer and he cried, "Lord, Lord,"
He laid down his hammer and he cried.

John Henry said to his captain,
"Captain, you go to town,
Bring me back a twelve-pound hammer, please,
And I'll beat that steam drill down, Lord, Lord,
I'll beat that steam drill down."

The captain said to John Henry,
"I believe this mountain's sinking in."
But John Henry said, "Captain, just you stand aside—
It's nothing but my hammer catching wind, Lord, Lord,
It's nothing but my hammer catching wind."

John Henry said to his shaker,
"Shaker, boy, you better start to pray,
'Cause if my twelve-pound hammer miss that
 little piece of steel,
Tomorrow'll be your burying day, Lord, Lord,
Tomorrow'll be your burying day."

John Henry said to his captain,
"A man is nothing but a man,
But before I let your steam drill beat me down,
I'd die with a hammer in my hand, Lord, Lord,
I'd die with a hammer in my hand."

The man that invented the steam drill,
He figured he was mighty high and fine,
But John Henry sunk the steel down fourteen feet
While the steam drill only made nine, Lord, Lord,
The steam drill only made nine.

John Henry hammered on the right-hand side.
Steam drill kept driving on the left.
John Henry beat that steam drill down.
But he hammered his poor heart to death, Lord, Lord,
He hammered his poor heart to death.

Well, they carried John Henry down the tunnel
And they laid his body in the sand.
Now every woman riding on a C and O train
Says, "There lies my steel-driving man, Lord, Lord,
There lies my steel-driving man."
—Anonymous

11

Poetry Pointers: Rhyme

Listen for **rhyme**. You can hear it. Rhyming words sound different at the beginning but alike at the end. What matters is the way the words are pronounced, not the way they are spelled. In the first stanza of "John Henry," *knee* rhymes with *me*. In the second stanza, *chest* rhymes with *rest*. Which words rhyme in the third and fourth stanzas?

Slant Rhyme

In stanza 5, *in* and *wind* do not quite rhyme. In stanza 7, *man* and *hand* do not quite rhyme. That almost-rhyme is called **slant rhyme** or near rhyme. Slant rhyme is often used in narrative poems. Look for another example of slant rhyme in "John Henry."

Repetition and Refrains

Many poems repeat a word or a phrase. When a group of words is repeated in a song, those words are called the **chorus**. In a poem, a group of words that repeat are called a **refrain**.

The words in "John Henry" repeat in two different ways. The fourth line of each stanza ends with the words "Lord, Lord." The last line of each stanza repeats the fourth line except for the last two words.

What does this repetition add to the poem?

But the words in line four and line five are not exactly the same in each stanza. Only the words "Lord, Lord" are repeated in each stanza of the poem.

Rhyme Schemes

A **rhyme scheme** is a way to describe a rhyming pattern. Each line in a poem is assigned a letter based on the last word in the line. All the lines that rhyme are given the same letter.

The word at the end of the first line is always given the letter *a*. Any end word that rhymes with that word (including slant rhymes and repeated words) is also given an *a*. The next end word that doesn't rhyme is given the letter *b*. Then every word that rhymes with that is also given a *b*, and so on.

The words at the ends of the lines in the first stanza of "John Henry" are *baby, knee, steel, me,* and *me*. Each stanza (without the repeating "Lord, Lord") uses the rhyme scheme **a b c b b**

Literature Link: Story Elements

Story Elements in "John Henry"

Character(s)	By some accounts, the character John Henry is more than six feet tall. In others, he is shorter and brawny. Tall or short, John Henry is so strong that he never gets tired. He is also determined to win at any cost. These traits, or characteristics, are qualities of a hero.
Setting	Where did this poem take place? People from several states say it was part of their history. The poem, however, does not name a specific place. John Henry sits on his mama's knee and then climbs a mountain to work. His body is carried down through a tunnel and laid in sand. The time is near the time of the invention of the steam drill.
Plot	John Henry competes against a steam drill, a new invention. He wins the race, but he loses his life in the process. People everywhere mourn his death.
Theme	The struggle of a human against a machine

13

Thinking Aloud

John Henry was a **legend**. That means his story came from history, but no one was exactly sure that it was true.

Kimberly and her group read the "John Henry" poem. Then they worked together to brainstorm some new characters. They made three different lists.

Write a biographical poem about something that happened in your own life!

Now It's Your Turn!

Are you ready to write your own poem? Think of someone you admire. You can choose a name from the students' brainstorming list. Then think about the person's achievements.

Don't try to fit the person's entire life into one poem. Focus on one event instead. It could be a big event or a small one. Just make sure you show the beginning, middle, and end. Add a little background information if you need it.

Legends
Johnny Appleseed
Paul Bunyan
Robin Hood
William Tell
King Arthur and
   the Knights of the
   Round Table

History
Rosa Parks
Martin Luther King, Jr.
Nelson Mandela
Amelia Earhart
Elizabeth Blackwell
Neil Armstrong

Sports
Jackie Robinson
Mia Hamm
Jesse Owens
Jackie Joyner-Kersee
Bonnie Blair
Roberto Clemente

A narrative poem does not have to rhyme. If you want to use rhyme, try it in every other line. Try to set up a regular rhythm. Break your poem into stanzas if you like. Use repetition if it fits.

Kimberly wrote a story poem about her friend.

When Ella Jumps Rope on the Playground

When Ella jumps rope on the playground,
everyone gathers around.
They count together every time
the jump rope hits the ground.

One day, her teacher came to watch
when the crowd called, "Ninety-three!"
The bell rang. Time to go inside,
but Ms. Brooks said, "Watch and see!"

The principal joined the gathering
when the crowd called, "Six hundred four!"
When her father came to take Ella home,
he watched her jump some more.

At fourteen hundred, the sun went down.
The light was fading fast.
When it grew too dark to see,
She put the rope down at last.

When Ella jumps rope on the playground,
everyone gathers around
helping her count and hoping to see her
jump till the sun goes down.

Chapter 3: Writing a Mysterious Narrative Poem

In this chapter, you will read, write, and recite a **mystery** story poem. A mystery is something that can't be explained. It might be spooky. It might be scary. Or it may just be a secret that someone else doesn't want you to know.

How do you write about a mystery? Let this famous poem guide you. Notice how the setting is described. The setting is both the place and the time in the story. In this poem, the words that describe the place and the time are very specific.

The Listeners

"Is there anybody there?" said the Traveller,
Knocking on the moonlit door;
And his horse in the silence champed the grasses
Of the forest's ferny floor:
And a bird flew up out of the turret,
Above the Traveller's head:
And he smote upon the door again a second time;
"Is there anybody there?" he said.
But no one descended to the Traveller;
No head from the leaf-fringed sill
Leaned over and looked into his grey eyes,
Where he stood perplexed and still.
But only a host of phantom listeners
That dwelt in the lone house then
Stood listening in the quiet of the moonlight
To that voice from the world of men:
Stood thronging the faint moonbeams on the dark stair,
That goes down to the empty hall,
Hearkening in an air stirred and shaken
By the lonely Traveller's call.
And he felt in his heart their strangeness,
Their stillness answering his cry,
While his horse moved, cropping the dark turf,
'Neath the starred and leafy sky;
For he suddenly smote on the door, even
Louder, and lifted his head:—
"Tell them I came, and no one answered,
That I kept my word," he said.
Never the least stir made the listeners,
Though every word he spake
Fell echoing through the shadowiness of the still house
From the one man left awake:
Ay, they heard his foot upon the stirrup,
And the sound of iron on stone,
And how the silence surged softly backward,
When the plunging hoofs were gone.
—Walter De La Mare

17

Ballad Form

The traditional ballad has four lines in a stanza.
Every other line rhymes, so the rhyme scheme is *abcb*.

The stanzas in this poem can be hard to see. That is because there are no spaces between them. But if you look carefully, you can see the rhymes in lines 2 and 4.

"Is there anybody there?" said the Traveller,
Knocking on the moonlit door;
And his horse in the silence champed the grasses
Of the forest's ferny floor:
And a bird flew up out of the turret,
Above the Traveller's head:
And he smote upon the door again a second time;
"Is there anybody there?" he said.

After four lines, the rhyme scheme starts over.

a
b
c
b
a
b
c
b

Alliteration

Are you ready to play with words? Can you write a line with words that all begin with the same sound? You can see "forest's ferny floor" and "silence surged softly" in this poem. That's called **alliteration**.

The rhyme in a ballad is not always perfect. Can you find the slant rhymes in this poem?

There are some other sound patterns you can try. You may want to repeat the same consonant in another place. Have some of the words in a line end with the same consonant sound. Or try it in the middle of several words in a line. Can you hear the *r* sound in "furry brown squirrel?" When consonants repeat in the middle or the end of several words in a line it is called **consonance**.

If you try this with vowels, it is called **assonance**. You can see it in these words: "wet yellow feather."

Story Elements in "The Listeners"

Character(s)

The main character, the Traveller, is not named. All we know of his appearance is that he has grey eyes. He rode a horse, and he knocked on a door that no one answered. He is described as "perplexed and still" and "lonely."

What can we infer from his actions? He thought someone was waiting for him. He came back because he had made a promise. He kept his word, so he appears to be reliable.

The other characters in the poem are "a host of phantom listeners." What do they add to the poem's mood?

Setting

The poem takes place at night. Look for words about stars, the moon, and moonlight. How many can you find?

There are more clues about the world of the story. Did you see "grasses of the forest's ferny floor," "lone house," "dark turf," "leafy sky," and "shadowiness"? How do these descriptions help you see the setting?

The house itself is described as having a turret, or a tower. It also has a "leaf-fringed sill." What kind of house does this sound like to you?

Plot

An unidentified man knocks on a door. No one answers, so he calls out a message. Then he rides away.

Theme

The theme might be "A promise is a promise." What do you imagine the Traveller might have promised? Why could he have been at the house? (No one knows for sure, so there are no wrong answers to this question.)

Thinking Aloud

Austin and his group brainstormed a list of setting details. They thought of words for all five senses. They were looking for words that seemed mysterious.

see
darkness
fog
storm clouds
shadows
movement
mysterious
message

taste
anything
unfamiliar or
unexpected

smell
someone's perfume
smoke

hear
weird noises
creaking door
animal sounds
spooky music
whispering voices
footsteps

feel
chill
goosebumps
breeze from an
open window
hair standing up

Write Your Own Mysterious Narrative Poem
Now It's Your Turn!

Where will your mystery take place? When will it happen? Think about the place and time of your story poem.

Make a list of possible places. You can use a desert, a mountain, a forest, or a farm. A city, a school, or a shopping mall might be on your list.

What details will you use to show the place? Will you write about the past, present, or future? How will your word choices show the time of day, season, or year?

Once you've placed your character in a setting, think about what might happen there. Is the setting safe or dangerous? How does your character feel about it?

Remember that readers want to find some excitement. A quiet setting in which not much happens can lead to a boring story. A poem might not have room for a huge problem, but try to create some tension to hold readers' interest. Austin wrote about going camping.

On a Misty Morning
One misty morning long ago,
well before the dawn,
we woke up early in our tent
and put our waders on.

We tromped through murky swampland,
deep and dark as night
to watch the sun come rising up
from a distant site.

Great horned owls hooted.
They echoed all around.
Then I heard an eerie
howling sound.

"What was that?" I whispered.
No one heard but me.
"No wolves near here," Mom answered.
What else could it be?

I guess I'll always wonder.
I may never know
what made that mournful howling sound
one day long ago.

Chapter 4: Writing a Fantasy Narrative Poem

Are you ready for some make-believe? In this chapter, you will read, write, and recite a **fantasy** story poem. Fantasy is one type of **fiction**.

When you write fiction, you make up what happens. Most fiction stories are like real life. The story isn't real, but it could be.

In a fantasy story, there is even more make-believe. What happens in a fantasy story could never happen in real life. Tables and chairs can talk. They can go for a walk. They can eat beans and bacon.

The Table and the Chair

I.

Said the Table to the Chair,
"You can hardly be aware
How I suffer from the heat
And from chilblains on my feet.
If we took a little walk,
We might have a little talk;
Pray let us take the air,"
Said the Table to the Chair.

II.

Said the Chair unto the Table,
"Now, you *know* we are not able:
How foolishly you talk,
When you know we *cannot* walk!"
Said the Table with a sigh,
"It can do no harm to try.
I've as many legs as you:
Why can't we walk on two?"

III.

So they both went slowly down,
And walked about the town
With a cheerful bumpy sound
As they toddled round and round;
And everybody cried,
As they hastened to their side,
"See! The Table and the Chair
Have come out to take the air!"

IV.

But in going down an alley,
To a castle in a valley,
They completely lost their way,
And wandered all the day;
Till, to see them safely back,
They paid a Ducky-quack,
And a Beetle, and a Mouse,
Who took them to their house.

V.

Then they whispered to each other,
"O delightful little brother,
What a lovely walk we've taken!
Let us dine on beans and bacon."
So the Ducky and the leetle
Browny-Mousy and the Beetle
Dined, and danced upon their heads
Till they toddled to their beds.
—Edward Lear

Edward Lear wrote this poem. He also made these drawings for it.

Poetry Pointers: Language

Edward Lear lived from 1812-1888. The language in his work reflects the time in which he lived. In "The Table and the Chair," the table complains of *chilblains*, a skin condition caused by exposure to cold. *Pray* in this context means *please*. To *take the air* means to go outside for a walk or ride.

Edward Lear used creative naming and spelling in his poems. He calls the duck a *Ducky-quack* to rhyme with *back*. He spells *little* as *leetle* to rhyme with *beetle*. What does he call the mouse? Why do you think he might have used that name?

Personification

In "The Table and the Chair," the table and chair talk. They also walk, dance, and sleep in beds. The duck, the mouse, and the beetle act like people, too. The poet wrote about each animal or object as though it was a person. This is called **personification**.

Character(s)

The characters include furniture and animals. A table and chair talk and move. A duck, a mouse, and a beetle help them find their way home. Who do you think "everybody" is?

Setting

The poem has a town and an alley. There is also a castle in a valley. In the end, they go back to their house. Where could these places be?

Plot

The table and chair take a walk and get lost. They hire help. Then they return home for dinner, dancing, and bed.

Theme

The table says, "It can do no harm to try." It's like the saying "Nothing ventured, nothing gained." Which saying do you think expresses the theme better?

Charlene and her group had some decisions to make. What kind of fantasy character did they want to write about? They had three choices. They could write about a human. They could write about an animal. Or they could write about objects like the furniture in "The Table and the Chair."

They talked about each choice. How could they write about a human?

"We have to make sure it is a fantasy," said Kimberly. "Maybe the character could have super powers."

"We can make an animal act like a person," said Austin.

"Does it wear clothes or talk?" asked Charlene.

"Make it act like an animal, too," said Kimberly.

"What about an object?" asked Charlene. "How does it act?"

Who is the character? What does it do in the story? Charlene made this **cluster** for her poem. She wrote her character in the middle. Then she circled it. She added words to describe it. She added actions, too. She added a circle for each new idea.

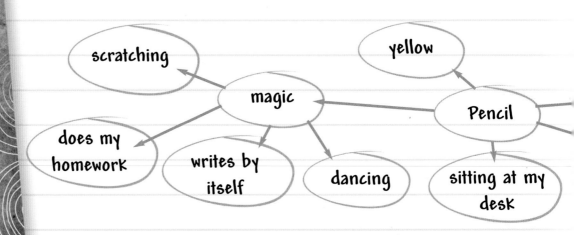

Write Your Own Fantasy Narrative Poem
Now It's Your Turn!

You can write about a fantasy character, too. Follow the steps that Charlene took. Decide what kind of character you want to write about. Then make a cluster to help you think. Who is your character? What will it do in the story?

After you make a cluster, it's time to organize it. What will happen first? Write a 1 in that circle. What is next? Put a 2 in that circle. Add numbers until you reach the end.

Now you are ready to write your poem. Here is what Charlene wrote for her first draft:

My Pencil Did My Homework
I stared at piles of homework.
I had to rest my eyes.
I heard a funny scratching sound
and got a big surprise.
My pencil did my homework.
It stopped when Dad walked by.
I acted like I was working hard.
I gave a great big sigh.
I'll never use a marker
or a ballpoint pen.
My pencil did my homework,
and it's doing it again!

Did you think of any new ideas? Add a new circle for each one. Give it a number, too.

In the next chapter, you can see how Charlene's classmates helped her revise.

pen → markers → eraser → paper → backpack

Dad comes over → close my eyes → pretend to work

Dad comes over → sigh

Chapter 5: Revising Your Narrative Poem

Congratulations! You have just completed the first two steps of writing. You brainstormed new ideas, then you used them to write your first draft. Now you are ready for the next two steps: revising and editing. Use this checklist as a guide.

Yes/No	Poem Elements	Yes/No	Story Elements
	Do the rhyming words rhyme well?		Do the characters fit the story?
	Does the rhythm match from line to line?		Is the plot logical?
	Can something repeat for greater effect?		Do setting details help show where and when events take place?
	Is any description specific?		Could a reader find clues to help determine the theme?

One good way to revise your poem is to share it with a group. Give each person a copy. Ask them to write their comments on it. Ask one person to read your poem aloud. Listen for any places where the reader stumbles with rhythm and rhyme. Give the others a chance to speak before you say anything about your work.

Then move to the next writing step. Did they see anything you need to edit? Are there any spelling, grammar, or punctuation errors?

Take time to think about every comment. Then use the ones that make the most sense to you.

The students read Charlene's poem out loud. Then they gave her some new ideas.

"You can break it into three stanzas," said Kimberly.

"I like that idea," said Charlene.

Austin helped Charlene improve the rhythm. He found something to change in each stanza. In the first one, she could add the word *till* to line 2. In the next one, she could use *pretended* instead of *acted like*. In the last one, she could change *ballpoint pen* to *fancy fountain pen*.

Charlene saw some verbs she could change. She changed *gave* to *sighed* and added some repetition to the poem.

Then she changed *got a big surprise* to *saw a sweet surprise*. That added alliteration to the poem. Here is her revised poem.

My Pencil Did My Homework

I stared at piles of homework
till I had to rest my eyes.
I heard a funny scratching sound
and saw a sweet surprise.

My pencil did my homework.
It stopped when Dad walked by.
I pretended I was working hard.
I sighed a great big sigh.

I'll never use a marker
or a fancy fountain pen.
My pencil did my homework,
and it's doing it again!

Chapter 6: Performing a Poem

The final step of writing is publishing your work. After you finish the final copy of your poem, you can share it with others. You can read your poem aloud to a group. You can perform your own poem!

You can also perform poems written by other poets. Choose a favorite and learn it by heart.

You can read a poem with a group. Recite the poem in **unison**. Read all of the lines together at the same time. Or take turns with the lines or stanzas.

You don't have to stop at the end of every line. Only stop if there is a natural break. Slow down if you see a comma. Stop for a bit when you see a period. Pause before you begin a new idea.

A narrative poem tells a story. So act it out! Whisper when it is scary. Raise your voice when things get exciting. Read faster or slower to show how the action is going. Have fun!

30

Learning More

Books

How to Write, Recite and Delight in All Kinds of Poetry by Joy N. Hulme and Donna W. Guthrie. Millbrook Press (2003)

John Henry by Julius Lester. Puffin (1999)

Vherses: A Celebration of Outstanding Women by J. Patrick Lewis. Creative Editions (2005)

Write a Poem Step by Step by JoAnn Early Macken. Earlybird Press (2012)

Websites

Children's Poet Laureate Mary Ann Hoberman reads from The Complete Nonsense of Edward Lear:
www.poetryfoundation.org/features/video/175

A short reading of Edward Lear's poetry.

Descriptive Writing with Virginia Hamilton:
teacher.scholastic.com/writewit/diary/index.htm

A helpful website which shows readers how to write using descriptive language.

Tips for Young Writers by Ralph Fletcher:
ralphfletcher.com/rf/?page_id=49

This website includes recommended tips and additional resources for budding young writers.

Glossary

Note: Some boldfaced words are defined where they appear in the book.

alliteration A series of words that begin with the same sound

assonance A series of words with the same vowel sound

cluster A brainstorming technique that links related words together

consonance A series of words with the same consonant sound in the middles and/or at the ends

drama A story meant to be performed as a play

fantasy A story that includes something that could not happen in real life

fiction A story about people and events that is not real

legend A story from history that people believe but can not prove

narrative A story

prose The language we speak and write every day

rhyme Identical sounds at the ends of words

rhyme scheme A system of describing the rhyming pattern of a poem or stanza

rhythm A pattern of regular sounds in a series of words

setting Time and place

slant rhyme Sounds at the end of words that are almost the same

stanzas Groups of lines in a poem

stressed Emphasized

tense The form of a verb that shows time as past, present, or future

theme The story's message

unison At the same time

Index